I0212469

The Innermost Sea

poems by

Nancy Avery Dafoe

Finishing Line Press
Georgetown, Kentucky

The Innermost Sea

Copyright © 2018 by Nancy Avery Dafoe
ISBN 978-1-63534-799-9 First Edition
All rights reserved under International and Pan-American Copyright Conventions.
No part of this book may be reproduced in any manner whatsoever without written
permission from the publisher, except in the case of brief quotations embodied in critical
articles and reviews.

ACKNOWLEDGMENTS

I would like to thank Leah Maines, Kevin Maines, and Christen Kincaid at Finishing
Line Press for publishing my book. I would also like to offer my deepest gratitude to
my daughters Colette and Nicole Dafoe, my son Blaise Dafoe, my sister-in-law Marilyn
Avery, dearest poet/writer friends Gwynn O'Gara and Jo Pitkin who wrote my blurbs
after reading my full manuscript. Many thanks, as well, to writers Mary Gardner, Karen
Hempson, Judith McGinn, Bobbie Panek, Sheila Byrnes, Cindy Hlywa, Janet Fagal, Joy
Kelleher, Georgia Popoff, and Barb Crossett who have all read and reread my work with
artists' eyes. I am deeply appreciative of Pen Women artists Katie Turner, Barbara Baum,
Joan Applebaum, and Wendy Harris who inspired some of my poetry and who allowed me
to use their artwork. I am also indebted to Susan Cerretani who inspired "Cultivating My
Antic Disposition."

"Returning to that Mineral State" first appeared in *An Iceberg in Paradise: A Passage through
Alzheimer's*, then the *English Record*, NYS English Council Journal, and most recently in
Poets Diving in the Night by the author.

"Entrance Exam" won the 2016 William Faulkner/William Wisdom creative writing poetry
competition.

"Red Blanket on a Line" was first published in *Insights* in 2017.

"Girl in the Hallway" won the CNY NLAPW poetry contest and first appeared on the CNY
Pen Women site.

"Child Who Would Not" first appeared on the *All We Can Hold* website in April 2017.

"A Turning" first appeared in the *Syracuse Post Standard*.

Publisher: Leah Maines
Editor: Christen Kincaid
Cover Art: Katie Turner
Black bird art: Barbara Baum
Author Photo: Parker Stone II Photography
Cover Design: Leah Huete

Printed in the USA on acid-free paper.
Order online: www.finishinglinepress.com
            also available on amazon.com

Author inquiries and mail orders:
Finishing Line Press
P. O. Box 1626
Georgetown, Kentucky 40324
U. S. A.

Table of Contents

Traveling Inward

Toward Perception

Steering with Scrutiny

Through Rumination

To Epiphany

for Daniel
for whom I wrote the first poem for him at age seventeen and
have been writing for him ever since

Closest we come to merging origins
of language and meaning,
memory retains its past lives

Traveling Inward

Innermost Sea

Between sea and shore, ethereal salt mist
becomes perceptible, water ascending,
rocks breaking boundaries and drifting
into the chimerical;
poet's tongue tasting brine in paint brush strokes
and water's breath;
age and ageless transfused through this permeation,
primary colors in collision within spray:
white, green, tertiary intensity beneath blue harmony,
form out of abstraction
almost in the way we imagine first creation:
suggestion is all the mind needs to call up
engagement of land and waterscape,
not a point, nor a line,
an experience
between divisions.
Salt on our skin, we are perplexed
about origins, returning to the sea;
rocks on shore and in our resolve.

We are water,
tossing about wildly.

Poem Registering in the Throat

Utterances given shape and sound, expelled
      in fury or sorrow;
Poet's search for the concrete and abstract,
         each trope
         unreeling
         naked and scarred
         from a tangled knot of language,
         parsed after landing on the page, slowly, elongated
         like vowels swallowing.

One poet stumbling over others; discovered
         in a basement bookstore—
         nothing shiny and new here, these rough gems
         ragged at the edges,
         worn covers showing signs of abuse
         in any other arena except reading,
         where that tear and stain, those fingerprints
         and smudges are a writer's lover,
         the reader knowing where to turn again,
         one page earmarked by a folded corner.

How long this little Cuban book stood languishing
         on a shelf, as if the verses inside
         weren't woven silk,
         their poetry spouting
         the revolution still new, excited voices
         heard as the book is opened.

One note claiming proud resistance,
         another suggests whispers from a jungle,
         "Poetica" jumps off the page entirely,
         running around the bookstore, inhaling loneliness.

Seeping through fabric of Cuban Spanish,
         with hints of Haitian Creole in the neighborhood,
         translations follow across the spread; facing one another
         this English consonant, that Cuban sonant.

Another poet claiming America has no right to poetry
        with her oppressor's bloody teeth,
        but this American oppressor oppresses her own,
        and poets emerge
                out from under the jackboot,
                waking and calling out
        from this amalgam of a nation.

Cuban poet writes, poetry of the many is poetry of one
        and one
        and one
        and one,
        crude,
        erudite,
        political,
        personal:
        all spondees,
        iambs,
        this Cuban Spanish
        like American English with its own character:
        here shallow,
        over there, pure depth,
        loud consonants and silent letters.

Leaving the bookstore, she finds
        a blind poet walks confidently down the street with a cane.
By a pillar, another poet leans with a poem
        in his pocket.
Like the Cuban revolutionary,
        he prefers to wear his poetry rather than assign it to shelves.

Poetry: currency for the living

Traveler between Stations

Pacing day and night in anticipation,
she listens near frosted window panes,
hearing only the silence of snow.

With stones in her pockets, she leans out,
following currents with her eyes closed,
writer's voice swallowed by wind.

Fourteen stations on route,
yet she has stopped at only a few
on her pilgrimage compelled by longing.

Her path appears to be meandering,
like the treks of Wordsworth and his lonely sister,
wordsmiths traversing fields of thought.

These sudden departures make her feel
exhilarant but terribly vulnerable
between stations and senses.

Chilled in that silent landscape,
always listening for a line,
observing a solitary tern overhead.

She wraps her scarf around her,
temperature changing her breath
to concentrated, visible air.

Dickinson in her pocket with small stones,
poet ghosts suggesting vehicles for a soul,
each journey paradoxically incomplete.

Stopped again before boarding,
she dreams with her chin resting on her palm.
What lies beyond sight lines and high dark?

Tranströmer in her pocket with icy winds,
near cold waters. She rises in a hot air balloon:
mortality signaling quietly below.

Bound

"The single and peculiar life is bound,
With all the strength and armour of the mind."
[Shakespeare, Rosencrantz in Hamlet,
Act III, sc. iii, l. 11-12]

Purposefully amnesiac yet bound
by language that falls out of rhythm
like coins or diamonds dropping
from her mouth in some forgotten
fairy tale altered by that imperfect
arbiter, memory, which shapes
conscious thought,
the ridiculous designer
of kingdoms and such stuff as tripping
down the stairs metaphorically,
not quite tragic
but neither is it slapstick;
entirely unaware
of inevitable confines that stop us
at an edge of the hyperbolic stage
on which we dance like small actors
immersed in ourselves
until falling into dust

In a Book's Spine

A book bent at its spine,
twisted backwards,
tumbles out words
in a line:
"Amber
upset
didn't
convinced
named
stood
William
who had
stolen
several
doubts"

Looking
for message in the randomness
of word spilling, like Ursula LeGuin's
speaker searching for signification
in froth on a beach,
kicked up by ocean tumult,
or the meaning
of intricate lines found
in a lace collar—
all these *"Texts"*
we're seeking to decipher
even when we know
questions will be
unanswered.

Conceit of Crows on Authorship

A Sonnet for Roland Barthes

Pontificating crows, forgetting their wings,
hopped along a country road and related canards,
all at once, of course, so their identities were things
fused in feathers, as well as sounds of grating bards
addressing aesthetic authority of collaborative authorship,
their raucous calls sung not in dispute but unison, designed
to confront opposing rhetoricians' claims on original script
of etymological sense of authority in assertion aligned
with unlimited text, "all derivative and contextual."
Startled by a shot, these black birds suddenly took to air,
a murder of crows arguing in "death of the author" dual,
contrasted with the single note and unusual flair

of a white-throated sparrow, "ridiculous songbird"
believed her voice, in deconstructed wind, was heard.

[Artwork by Barbara Baum]

Geography of Obsession

A single Monarch butterfly alights
    leaving the Sierra Madres in Mexico
        and within moments, it begins again.

A great migration, spanning four
    generations, all imprinted with some
        journey deeper than memory; we travel:
    these flights
        in which neither bird, nor insect,
            nor fish, nor reptile, nor mammal
                is individual but rather part of collective
    will shifting or fluttering yet somehow
        linear in following routes, dictated
            by the undecipherable, those codes
          orchestrating wing or fin, trunk or foot
              into abstruse patterns swallowing
           themselves, releasing again and again
           undistractable thought across
    thousands of miles, impulse after impulse
        retrieved from bottled energy,
    this assemblage,
        this darkening of skies or sweep of continents,
        this eminent combining.

"Poetry is too damned intimate,"

       said Sam three rows back.
"The trouble with poetry,"
       Billy Collins wrote,
"is that it seems to cause / the writing of more poetry."
       but I think the trouble lies
elsewhere with that "imperial jointress"
       from *Hamlet*, her ripped seams,
or an open shirt that catches us
       unaware when a poet refers
to his alcoholic breath, his naked
       "Danse Russe," or threatens
to open a vein, surprising
       with veracity. Even when singing
about our carpenter, mason, girl-sewing
       America, Whitman still embarrasses
with his wildly delicious, sensuous
       open-mouthed language, words
formed by probing tongue licking
       salt from skin, poet loitering until
we close our doors or allow him
       or her to settle in with us
          for a night.

Returning to that Mineral State

I

Something about a stone, a stone,
a stone—when my nephew placed
little colored rocks on marbled
gravestone that marked where my
brother lay, it wasn't a tradition
I knew, but one that was comforting,
so, I continued to bring him white
quartz and red-veined granite
from shores near our cabin, where
I found myself searching for stones
then thinking of the past as we kids
smashed shale slabs, peering inside
mysteries, and we pressed fingers
into indentations,
feeling ridges left by shells
harboring ancient lives, and it seemed,
when I was young,
that a stone could talk.

II

Carrying a smooth, black pebble
for luck, I rubbed it long, seeing again
my brother watching me skimming
a stone across lakes, opposing forces holding it
seemingly forever.

III

I find I fit inside a W.S. Merwin stone
poem, recognizing Beckett and Shakespeare
and Kenyon who gave her dog a stone rather
than a bone, and Wilfred Wilson Gibson
who sought out stones,
and Margo Berdeshevsky whose book

Between Soul and Stone resides
in this density.
Turning it over and over in my palm—
this stone could take our worry, mark our dead,
record our time—slips and skips
across open water,
until all that is left
is a stone,   a stone,   a stone.

Toward Perception

Recalling Blind Beach

No Oedipus stumbling about here at Blind Beach;
rather, dogs—big Black Mouth Curs, fawn-colored,
descend rapidly, easily, over perilous rocks,
stone falling away from cliffs to the black and gray
spectrum of pebbles and finely broken, empty shells,
this shoreline where fog and clouds come in low,
deceive the eye in this place of concealment
near the Russian River outlet to the sea.
South of Goat Rock, we stand silently
in awe of Arch Rock, offshore sentry warning us
of hidden outcroppings, skerries, and low sea stacks
along Sonoma's rugged coastline.

Off Highway 1, we follow Goat Rock Road down
its winding, narrow path past sunset boulders,
from another geologic time when plate collisions
violently gave birth. No swimming, the warning:
rip currents disguised in this wild mouth harboring
harbor seals, kelp beds, fragile life in the sea.

Mammoths once tramped above this shoreline;
now, German Shepherds, Pit Bull Terriers,
a pair of Doberman Pinschers peacefully dominate
pebble beach, leaping over colossal, beached tree trunks,
those skeletal remains of giants washed up, left behind,
like the Russians who once logged old forest near the river.

Descent is tricky; we climb over what looks like eye-sockets
of a leviathan, finding it is only an uprooted redwood, hole left
by knots in waterlogged wood, but it reads as skeletal remains
drawn up from other ages; early beasts surprising man
who had crossed an inhospitable continent to take in
his lungs the chill, moist air of the antipodal.

Acuity

Long, straight line division—
blue above, black below—like imagined
boundary of horizon holding water and sky,
only blacker water below is far below,
deeper than phantasm of clouds moving
in waves suggesting vastness to leap into
and start swimming, but instead, you would drop
37,000 feet before hitting and exploding.

Wings pitch dark with lights at the tips—
puny and seemingly insignificant—not enough
to light the way but enough to suggest a pulse.
Demarcation between land and sky—
only the other country you see is vapor,
and the line is curve of the earth and
not straight at all, and as for the sky, well,
it is void you can only imagine.

Entrance Exam

Listening while traveling in an art gallery,
a voice whispers from the canvas
of a John Singer Sargent painting;
it is not the artist but his 17-year old niece
Rose-Marie Ormond sighing deeply,
aware of the end of opulence and indulgence
as world war looms in the still distance,
this beautiful young woman
to die in a church bombed by the Germans
only a few years after she gave movement
to repose in *Nonchaloir.*

"The models must be paid," Vincent Van Gogh
said to his brother Theo—moving his eye
along textured, blanched oils of symbolization
on an absorbent canvas. There must have been
something about her, however, more than texture
as he painted her again and again,
first in whites then blues.
Did she sense his calm before desperation?
Did she intuit, even for an instant
he was about to blow a hole in his chest,
or perhaps be murdered?
Was she wholly unaware of "light on light"
before deepest darkness? Was she aware
that we were watching her, too?

"Cousine," Fantin-Latour says, as he reaches for oils
to contrast with white and yellows delicately mixed as her dress.
He is thinking not of his mother's side now,
that spirited Russian in his blood,
but Sonia knows all this and will never betray him,
will hold her lips delicately closed without speaking,
hour after hour until the still-life painter
of flowers has captured her as *une fleur.*
All these years later, she is speaking to us
now, no longer silent but still composed.

We wander into the room where
she waits, not Matisse's first Odalisque
nor his last, this girl of 19 when she first
said, "yes, I will model for you," dressed
only in gold belt and diaphanous skirt
that is not skirt at all, rather texture of fog
burnt off in late morning.
Henriette Darricarrere encloses her own face
with angular arms as she sits in a chair
that surrounds her: frames within frames
like a mystery she promises not to expose.
Red, red, red floor, walls, her lips,
then green stripes on yellow chair:
color, form, outline—Fauvist style,
deliberate distortion. Her head too small,
she thinks without contempt or criticism
when she finally looks at his painting
not of her, not her life, not her love
but an intensity of color, shapes,
she inspires, so intimate she believes
a canvas begun in flirtation could end
feeling like rape.

Degas labors over caliginous bronzed, muscular
figurine, with its lush shadow, more defined
than anything else on canvas, including
the subject, Madame Camus initially unaware
of Degas' caress of statue in its golden wrap,
suggesting silk, more substantial than she
as blurred image, woman become form,
pigments at her neck and bosom,
mystification rather than the artist she is,
her fingers light on keys of a piano, as light
as brush strokes of her husband's friend.
She strokes her wedding band out of tensile
boredom until Edgar commands she hold
her hands silent while brush touches

strip of gold with glint of departing light,
Degas layering cardinal, and Madame Camus
remembering what her husband
has told her about his brilliant friend:
artist obscuring subject while aware
of losing his sight but not his vision.

In another room, the women do not come and go,
like T.S. Eliot's women, "talking eruditely and politely."
They are flesh and blood lovers, friends,
artists trying to find a way in a man's
art world where we watch closely as Amedeo Modigliani
wraps his arms around her supple body,
his warm hand caressing her naked breast;
she must have startled at her portrait
that was not portraiture at all but,
rather, provocation, contrived with corrupted shapes,
precocious colors, incorporeal debauchery
holding fantastical surprise. Then, she, rather than he,
turns and passionately kisses the man
who would teach her,
blind to the tragedies waiting.

Red Blanket on a Line

Fire outside a window—
No, not fire—
sunlight flaming in furious folds
of red blanket flapping on a line
in November winds
mistaken before image is processed,
nerve fibers crossing over;
covering catching and releasing light
like waves cresting where tempests
claim domain, or a river kidnaps light,
rushing us along
in cold bewilderment.

Inside, a black bat with folded,
wide wings,
creature verses mystery in a corner
where ceiling meets north wall at acute angle.
No, not bat—
it is only shadow shaped
by rising light caught and held
at oblique angle.

Distortions of light on light,
dark on dark,
aberrations when our occasionally hapless
biology is master, thinking we are loved
when there is only lust in the temporal lobe.
No, not quite—
it seems, preoptic area
is also involved in this give and take.
Love now conducting an aria
in our brains playing the drums,
cello, flute, piccolo, bassoons, horns
and harp at just the right
musical moment.

Look, a child.

No—
a young man waits
in shadow, slowly striding into light,
perplexity found in that family of birds'
optical illusion or one where a woman
is also word in elegant script.

In search of meaning as image forms
on retinas, all those rods and cones
converting to impulse,
considered by that intelligent reader
who loves a good book in our brains:
error after error in a lifetime of conceits.

Corresponding Collisions

It's simple, really:
we're all looking for truth.

Searching inside energy, within metaphors
where poetry, physics, philosophy, chemistry,
history, mathematics, the arts, and astronomy
collide and change in the lambent rays we hold them.

Euclid, Coleridge, Newton, Calvino, Rayleigh, Neruda—
examining wavelengths of light in various orders—
students scattered at the far end, unsure, confused.
Encourage them not to stop mixing science, history,
mathematics, poetry, science, literature
symmetrically, of course.

Symmetry deliberate: chiasmus, too,
between matter and energy, the matter a pun
created to challenge, see how each concept resonates,
another play on the way we function, seeing the function;
so, the scattering corresponds to molecular spectroscopy:
we're absorbed in what may have been born
in Newton's optics, but we find our way
poetically in this energy transfer

from teacher to student, student to student,
student to teacher, teacher to teacher,
our processes dynamic, resonant frequency resonates
within our rational, artistic, philosophical souls,
in which we calculate our losses, build upon
progress, as well as reveal truth in white light.

Albino Alces Alces

We could hear a pair of loons in the distance,
our small motor struggling, Lac Yser's water
gurgling around the propeller of a little boat,
wind only just picking up and carrying
human scent when we spotted him on shoreline,
coming out of tall grasses where he had been feeding.

His long legs betrayed him, his confusion causing him
to double back over a narrow strip between rocks
and water—that hard place. Born in the spring,
he appeared a ghost at the end of summer.
An all-white coat confounding as we struggled
to identify before he returned to the density
of forests, only his tracks in sand left the impression
we had not imagined this incongruity.

In Tanzania and Burundi, children born
with oculocutaneous have been sacrificed for their body
parts in spite of laws forbidding the practice. Cultures
and nature have not done well with anomalies.

In the rarest of sightings, finding a young moose
on shoreline was 100,000 times rarer due to his lack
of pigmentation, and yet we were privileged to be there
at that exact moment when he lost his bearings.

Outside the standard norm and convention,
this young phenomenon was at one end of this scale,
applied by humans, a monstrosity—and at the other,
all the way to spiritual, blessed wonder.

Girl in the Hallway

For a moment, we were walking in a straight line,
as if in cadence: girlhood to maturity.
I deliberately slow my gait, not in pursuit;
I see pretty girls every day and scarcely notice,
trying instead to coax them into learning,
caught up in complexities, sometimes pitying
teen angst and spectacles enacted, entirely unaware
of epiphany that awaits not student but teacher.

Like Keats' *Cold Pastoral*, a scene across
intervals of time and generations, the woman
clever enough for allusions and pretensions,
self-reflexively, self-consciously indulgent:
romance out of academia
and "Ode on a Grecian Urn."

Then without warning, this shock: the self
metaphorically and literally heavier with age,
a curse not fine wine, softened in a sallowing.
But on this last day of school, I see her: this impossibility
of elusive beauty and truth just beyond reach.

Impressionism

Offering a mutable language,
blurred figures

                on a distant,
weathered dock

      materialize
as an Impressionist painting
that recedes
      then ripples,
           fluidity of the tableau
                reflected in the glow on water.

A diminutive dog
      is easier to discern
      for his sound effects.

           A willow tree forms
           an inconstant arch,   framing the scene
                wanting
              only the water lilies
                of Monet.

"Classical Head," 1922

Here Olga, first wife, is Classical;
later, it has been intimated, he would
paint her as a horse, as a hideous beast
of anatomical nightmare parts—breasts
like engorged worms and pointed teeth
wrapping around where a face should
have been--but that would be several
years away, after he had become
angry with his Ukrainian Russian,
jealous wife, whose beauty was never
apparent except in her grace
in the company of dancers, the one who ran
off and lived with him in Paris, unafraid,
but, here, Olga Khokhlova—after
giving birth to his son—tilts her head
in Classic posture like a Greek bronze
or marble sculpture, he tells her, before
destroying any thought of those
materials with the softness
of the mark-making on surface
of canvas: thick, tenebrous brown
curve of textured line, stylized,
accenting her face. Her curling
hair is pulled back and up to look
like a coif but not severely;
rhythm of wavy blurs all softness
and rounded like shape
of her right shoulder, her chin
rounded, too, as translucent
oils connote gauze floating
over her breasts; space around
her a layer of impasto, daubs
of browns deeper in tonality
near the top of her head, moving
into yellowish hues as they
approach mid-length of her
right arm, finally curving in

toward her body; brushes'
gestures hugging her close.

His portrait almost too facile, you
might walk right by in a rush
to reach the "Family of Saltimbanques,"
but you adjust your pace, turn back,
no, are pulled, stand and meet
not gaze of her downcast eyes
on Paulo—unseen infant son—
but her mouth which betrays
signification not of sex nor lust
nor even love; it is semblance of pout,
her lips prophetic, already dimly aware
of some far, French beauty
who will
capture the imagination
of her Picasso.

Eyes of Women

Mirrors of beauty, backbone, and burdens,
disembodied eyes can only be seen from above,
as if, indeed, the artist JR laid down his canvas
on top of rail cars to challenge the gods
with sundered images
from the back of his camera lens.

Women's eyes—indistinct in motion,
rushing, rumbling, dizzying journey along rails,
one car after another—read then weep
in rhythmic union. In focus, out of focus—
seeing abstracted—these totems compel, propel,
in the wake of what it is to be human
on tracks across Africa,
the wide back of our planet.

Disappeared

Between lines, below rippling surfaces,
something or someone has disappeared.

In our love of mystery lies an escape
out of a jail cell, some formidable fortress,
from a maze, Daedalus' elaborate Labyrinth.

Our schemes are symbols for *The Human Condition,*
such as Nemerov portrayed with his lonely man in motel room,
or Patrick Modiano's sixteen-year-old *Missing Person*
receding from the darkened streets of Paris.

Native Americans offered *l'itoi,*
neither ascent nor descent, the Leaving provides
no clues: only invisible trails of dissipating breath,

neither withdrawal nor avoidance, not desertion,
not loss here but rescue
from presence, from the present.

Saint James Triad

One bare leg audaciously draped
        over a cool metal frame,
      a naked foot
          dangling,
              a sensuous arm
                  curled
            round a straight line.

Women whose lives appear utterly
        unknowable, yet they sit as
           comfortably as mother and daughters,
without the need to verbalize connections,

        each with her bronze eyes eternally indifferent
        to the other world from which
           their boundaries were formed.

Steering with Scrutiny

Suddenly Elemental

"Look at the natural world,"
says my student Kazimieras,
"Circles, curves; everything is
rounded, even birth. Then man
comes along and conceptualizes
the world as flat."

"Man making declaration,
God-like," I state.

"And he arrives on scene, coming up with square,
with architecture," Kaz adds.

"How hard it was to let go of this idea--flat world...
How did Galileo dare?" I pose.

"But everything around him is round,"
 Kaz says smiling. "This is why I love physics,"
he continues by noting similarities between
sub-atomic particles and collective movements
of herding mammals, of flocking birds.

A moment later, Kaz turns his attention
to an ekphrastic poem, inspired by a painting
of a red-haired woman curled up in covers of swirling blue.
"Reminds me of Pamuk's novel, *The Black Book,*" Kaz states.

It reminded me of "Flaming June" by Lord Leighton, but
this is another painting, deeply saturated. Through
the power of Kaz's suggestion, I instantly consider character
Blue in Pamuk's novel *Snow,* but I should have known better,
only realizing, much later, how many of Pamuk's novels
are imbued with the character of paintings.

I leave Kaz's desk
and return later during class to watch him
create four, side-by-side columns.

"Why columns of words?" I ask.

"I was thinking of four classical elements; looking at her hair, I see fire. I recognize this painting. I mean, I haven't seen it, but I've read this description."

I suggest he give the columns
headings of the Greek Classical Elements.

He shrugs. "It's a work in progress," he says lightly.
All poems are works in progress, Kaz suggests
as the bell rings, and his images and our abbreviated
conversations hang in air along with poems
I thought I'd finished, a painting of a woman
suddenly elemental. I see her red hair burst
into flamboyant yet unquenchable flames,
antithetically floating on rolling seas of blue,
and I suddenly notice square windows through
which I look out, observing angularity:
desks,
room,
cabinets;
student teaching teacher how to regard
again, coming
round yet
again.

Younger Woman, Older Man

Lilt to her exaggerated laughter,
excited clicks of pouty, red high heels—
Still, freckles on her face and breast,
her nipples pretending to be insolent, he thinks
    "Maybe I?"
    "No.
    "We can't go 'round"

After all, he was no boy with nervous hands,
no tremor in his voice, a register deeper
than when he was sixteen.

    She could be his daughter but
    that would be incest;
    her lower lip pierced like his heart
    he mused, by now, knowing
    well enough where to hold his palm,
    moving his fingers around
    the small of her back,
    a coastal town he would inhabit.

His hair sandblasted, gray and white,
age running in tributaries
and spreading across his famous face,
down around his neck,
partially covered by his button-down collar,
his tie already carelessly thrown across chair,
but mother of pearl in his cufflinks
read immaculate, confident, successful,
    and he was done with penance:
    "Venial offense," he'd told his soon to be ex-wife.

Her slender fingers, an odalisque
suggestive in repose.

    Glances and turning heads,
    aspersions cast, snickering around the room.

"My God, how the hell? And she's—"
"How much older? What she sees in him—"
"Has to be about money—"
"He's famous—"
"In whose circles?"

All synecdoche, he considers, parsing her lips,
  hips, breasts, hands, thighs, the slit between her long legs
  like slant rhyme, he smiles to himself, familiarizing.
  "Fucking redemptive," he said out loud, and she turned
  as if shot in black and white film:
  gauzy, hazy, last scene in an old movie.

Still, he is thankful, no, much more,
as he holds an invisible tether,
a tether she passes between her teeth,
wraps around her thighs and pulls him toward her,
hearing the gossip in the room, and wanting
what she wants.

Cultivating My Antic Disposition

(a poem for two voices)

Why must poetry be so dead serious all the time?

A red feathered head stuck out of the entrance
of a birdhouse; two puncture holes where its eyes
once observed. Only Cardinal knew the full tragedy
but could no longer feel or articulate its metallic clip
of alarm; bird reduced to passive apparatus
in buffoonery, put-on, prank.

When the back door to the house is opened
and a passerby looks up, this diminutive scene
awaits remark: "Oh," in surprise, roundness
of her mouth, unconsciously mimicking birdhouse
opening, the way now blocked, moving us from
beautiful natural world to natural macabre one.

The ubiquitous, "Can't you take a joke?"

Perhaps there is none better than Shakespeare
at coaxing humor out of death,
his Grave Diggers speaking in puns,
both wittily and unwittingly,
the gambit of punning on arms
at once cleverly ridiculous and grotesque.

I think I know where you're going with this.

Contrivance of the caper—Cardinal, the cat's prize,
bantam bird decapitated, then rescued, stuffed in opening—

Rescued? Really? Going for absurdity, but start again—

After the cat abandoned its prey, a man
picked it up, considered inconsiderable loss,
then decided to poke its tufted red head into the hole

in jest or gambol, as Hamlet says.

Shall we undertake a discussion on the undertaker?

This clowning a cousin to Dante's caprice
in casting his political enemies into Hell:
"And the leader made a trumpet of his ass,"
wrote Robert Pinsky in translation,
one sardonic poet to another, and one barbed,
flayed sinner apparently, formerly employed as barrister.

*Hey, doesn't the word Cardinal also mean
essential, first, foremost, fundamental?*

Foremost, is the caper on Death with a capital,
Dante looking on as Virgil guides him
past awful torments of former tormentors,
but in his passages, we find ourselves smiling
in the midst of this boiling Inferno.

There is a little death every second of every minute of every life.

For a contemporary take on black humor in death,
Donald Antrim gives us a sacrificial Corn King—
favored brother—whose flesh is sliced as his brothers beat
and cut him, then obediently, compassionately close windows
as he tells them he is cold: death restoring order
in *The Hundred Brothers* and our diminutive birdhouse.

I presume you have others ready to recite?
Samuel Beckett's Waiting for Godot—
*Remember that bit about hanging themselves on a branch
that might hold the weight of one but not the other—*

Behind it all, threat that is not threat—
bright, decaying bird is Prince Hamlet at the end of the play;
poor bird with its missing eyes, detached body

is all of us eventually, so we laugh or cry
but, if it's all the same, would rather laugh.

Lighten up, will you?

Kay Ryan in "Shipwreck" suggesting,
arriving at that point, treating our sleight of hand
or mind, those articulations separating us from hope—
Shakespeare's and David Foster Wallace's *Infinite Jest*—
Howard Nemerov's young lovers accidentally
surprising a dead fish, its eyes still intact.

*Some of us prefer to laugh at, rather
than surrender to, that skeletal head*

We'll keep our keen eye
out for the absurd—
the space we occupy for the moment
which will be reversed,
T.S. Eliot suggested, not at all in jest,
and we sigh collectively and severally.

Cadaverous just a cat away.

Old Town

Gray flutter of pock-marked awning
gestures feebly as he walks past
blacked out windows silenced by brown papers;
only a few remnants of chipped, gold lettering left over
from another era when someone bounded up stairs
to the second floor.

Paper cups rolling furiously away
as if escape is still possible.
The only new store, a dollar store
with its flashing neon, OPEN sign.
A pizza shop hustler runs out into night,
hot and greasy boxes in a van rounding a corner.
Boarded up doors, store fronts wearing masks
from another dance; hard, cold, old brick
loosened from facades, lines fading.

Cigarette butts lay in rows between uneven sidewalk squares.
A favorite shoe store gone. Its sign lingers;
losses not violent but slow like an anchor
dragging muddy bottom.

Pervasive gray,
even the sun turning its head away,
long streets and buildings huddle in shadow.
Parking lots nearly empty, small city yanked
along on its belly, scarred and yet bleeding
after too many nights of abuse.
The worst: an animal carcass left on the street,
remains of sickness picked at by pigeons
and a lost gull. Christmas lights oddly turned on
in the sullen March night.

Smoking, Drinking Flarf

I.   **Prodigal**

Visions clearly
anti-scholarly garbled
detachment, escape
memory engineered
accelerated dreamily
meditation classification
silly thing, thing ting
language hostage
focus on anxiety, denial
screaming invited
then walked down
not indifferent: impotent;
couldn't shake technique,
punctuation either

II.   **Smoking, Drinking Flarf**

Filtered stray English
forget asserting
motion as well as momentum:
stars between cars;
green river bruised
against muted ochre.
Style lob
links lament deported:
smoking, drinking half-brothers,
theory of lovely
kicked out
the door

III.   **From Yesterday's News**

The German question:
historic mistake close-up;
the New York question:

wrongful death;
what's new?
Years after the killing,
we don't settle
plunged into darkness
performance art at the end
a sugar cane field and tunnel
entry into her country
walkabout then exodus
Op-ed sneaky, snarky—both;
review, review, review
vision exhibition collision

Joel said,

"Poetry is for women, and I hate poetry!"
I said, "You're right, poetry is for women
like Emily Dickinson and Elizabeth Bishop,

But poetry is also for guys who like sex
with women and guys who like sex with other guys,
and guys who just like sex

Like Frank O'Hara who wrote about
vandalism of our emotions and a poem
called "Beer for Breakfast," and about Vermouth
and veal, and I'll leave out the part
about what happens in his bathroom in a poem.

And Joel, poetry is for guys who shoot guns
and go off to war like Randall Jarrell and W.H. Auden
who wrote about art as our direct connection
to the dead and a poem called "Here War is Simple."

Poetry is also for Welsh guys like Dylan Thomas
whose nerves were wired on the page
and Russians like Pushkin who wrote
about Moscow's rivers of blood,
and Spanish guys like Lorca who wrote
of worms and stars in the same breath.

So, you're right, Joel,
poetry is for women,
but you're only half right..

Interiority

Mother needed a ride home
from third coast to the east coast.

The funeral director, a man with a bushy
mustache and big, soft palms, said, "Don't worry.
"We'll get her back here. We do this all the time."

Then I was looking out the window,
the wing silvering, wondering
who was flying in the belly of this plane,
body chilled in the cavity, wrapped for burial?

Even after landing, I continued to look
up at aircraft, considering again
mothers and fathers, sons and daughters,
husbands, wives, and lovers circling
above us in that other, interstitial chamber,

the one so narrowly separating the living
from the dead, their allegiances no longer
to the observable, finite world, yet here
they are among us, seemingly volitant,
embodying enigma, compelling
our emotional vistas.

Black Hole Cargoes

Singularity at Black Hole's heart,
      its one-way membranes marking
            cataclysmic deaths of stars.

This highly concentrated mass,
      with its intense indifference to suffering,
            due to its paradoxical density,

                  offers extinguishing of possibilities
            inherent in a planet's sphere; it suggests all kinds
            of metaphoric placeholders of possibility and impossibility.

Language and the seemingly preposterous
      about to meet at the point
            of annihilation made definitive

      by a lonely Hubble wandering
            in immensity of space as we read
                  its mind, and it indifferently considers

            negation of all life
                  on a planet as commonplace
                        in this immensity.

Scientists emboldened by paradox and
      ability to see that which cannot be seen
            but rather inferred from effects

            on matter or that which matters.
     while poet notes puns, irony,
            absurdity in the fact: there may be millions of them,

            thereby initiating energy so intense
            that nothing can escape their most terrible
            velocity: singularity meeting predictability.

[Although a poem may be read in any fashion by readers, this poem is intended to be read the way the eye takes in an arch: moving from the bottom left column up to the top and then across to the right column and down.]

Archer Bends a Bow

This symbol holding praying hands,
there again in the archetype.
stacked arches of history—
multi-foiled or leaved, transverse arch,
one found in Istanbul, once Constantinople,
One ancient and Celtic in origin,
the haunch on the other side.
filling in from keystone down
camera lens leading to symmetry
a brush stroke, a pencil line,
in stone: permanence and movement;
where mind completes this paradox
rising further north to crown,
up, up to the *voussoir,*
Eye following from impost to stilt,

hands no less sacred
for their pagan roots;
covert mystery already
in the curve before contour
we create suggested by the dome.
Progress slow, choral strophe:
magnificent architecture through
which refugees and their assassins
flee, passing death foreshadowed.
This portal supporting bridge,
bestows a window into history
looking into our art and artifice,
natural and unnatural portico
before contour we create:
archer bending low.

Blue Moon

I must have looked up at the moon
a thousand times and never seen
him as he was tonight, smiling in delight
with a mouth in an O for whistling
wild to be so personified,
lively and full of himself,
racing spectral clouds,
this man of a moon spiffed up in his rare Blue Moon
suit, commanding from the blackness of space
the waters of earth from opposition
in this gravitational, ancient attraction,
like the draw of two lovers in one;
our Moon Man's mien expressing no thought
of astronomy nor reflection on his crater-scarred face
no, only his paradoxical, antithetical light and dark
being as he continued his journey:
on and on, this tendency of flight
past billowy mass, on and on
and on into night.

Through Rumination

Lamentations

Pulling me in—
—Book of the Bible: Old Testament. *Lamentations of Jeremiah.*
 Note on act of expressing grief.
                    Grief,
                    personified Grief as city,
                    as woman
          1: *How doth the city sit solitary*
          2: *among all her lovers she hath none to comfort her*
          3: *My strength and my hope perished.*
          5: *We are orphans*
          Absence of 4.
          Absence
          We are orphans—
          implications if God with a capital is father?
          Patriarchal.
          Poets of the Bible, personifying city. Old poets.
          Yet we are orphans.
          With slow drawl—not slow—already incorporated in word drawl
unless redundancy becomes emphasis—seas or Sea?
          Begin suggesting life. Only later, eventually epochs,
          tumult without cessation.
          Exploration
                    Incorporation.
          Lovelorn city; "solitary" city,"
                    city without inhabitants, without voice, without ebb and flow,
                     city that was dead—yet not really past tense—not yet
                    accepting inevitable defeat

          I see this city. Correction: only this city—*the city sits solitary.*
          They all fit; none is suited.
          Destroy these notes tomorrow or the next day.
          Nothing to be seen.
          Nothing.
          Absence.

Worth Dying For

"Are some things still worth dying for"
in this all too jaded, cynical land
of disappearing opportunities and hope?

David Foster Wallace asked this prescient
question in *The Atlantic* a year or so before
apparently answering in the affirmative,
taking his own life, but leaving us with more
questions and sadness,
and it's not as if he hadn't thought about pain
even *Consider(ing) the Lobster*
as it struggled to claw its way out,
making desperate noises just as cook exits;
this writer, philosopher prince, this Hamlet
whose answer leaves us with awful perplexity
even as we're speculating whether or not
he knew precisely why
at the moment he held up a rope
long after he held up and studied the skull of America
and asked tragically, ironically,
bitingly, humorously, knowingly about
our "Infinite Jest."

Was it harder to imagine because
he created a body of rational work
amongst allusions and symbolizations epic
in nature, across and around waters all the way
to the Pacific from the shores of Cayuga?

Are we stalled at his final act or this writer's
pyrotechnic verbal display accessing humanity's
immortality and immorality even as he denied it?
Hadn't he been crowned like the Prince of Denmark?

And so, as if there was a logical consequence
to pretending too long that living in this world
is really a reasonable condition,

David Foster Wallace took his life,
leaving us Shakespeare's phrase
on sardonic lips of every tormented Hamlet,
finishing, of course, with "the rest is silence,"
somewhere offstage as we stand on deserted roads
wearing only Lucky's hat, reading nothing
more than Samuel Beckett's recycled, cyclical
directions: "They do not move."

They Call it "Car Guantánamo"

Scarred shoulders bleeding
rust behind razor wire:
impounded fenders,
blue chrome, slowly turning
acid white
in unrelenting
heat;
rats running through with immunity,
once interrupted, now
discontinued,
dreams.

Driving
even a clunker fast
to anywhere in the night—
counterpart
to tyranny.

Mortals

Their ache—80 feet up in the air,
the eastern white pine
groans against the tangled
blue-green needles and
dark-gray limbs of another
deeply furrowed voice—
is pronounced as the wind
insinuates itself then pulls
these prodigious mortals,
who sweat resins and
drop their cones that hit
the earth like pointed stones,
until their arms, rubbed raw,
register full complaint—
a long, low groan,
then a stretched-out
syllable, almost a spoken
word, clearly articulated
in the middle of the night.

The Interview

At the start, all is well-intentioned—interviewer
formulating questions in order to generate, produce,
capture but never control response—subject
never passive even when motionless, his or her eyes
offering bounty—if only that subtle look
could be converted to notations on a page.

Plimpton's exchange with Hemingway
exposed a gun in the room, readers knowing
hunter who was literary giant intended
to use his weapon, so the space lay as insinuation
even bookended by Hemingway's wit, his sarcasm
another weapon—his plain-spoken words a guise.

Donald Hall, already well-established poet
and editor of *The Paris Review* at the time,
gave T.S. Eliot a line or two to let it play out;
Eliot, however, refused to be reeled in, dropping
his guard only to retreat and his "I" becomes
"one," incisive over a "point" to be made.

Dorothy Parker—in her manteaux
of weary sophistication—tossed acerbity,
reducing the role of interviewer with sweet,
oh, so sweet, unmistakable condescension: "dear,"
"my dear," and "honey" dripping on S.J. Perelman
from her honeycomb of smart, cynical banter.

Ted Hughes carefully crafted responses showing
control of a man and poet reserved until
Drue Heinz asks, "Would you talk about burning
Plath's journals?" Obfuscation then reversal:
"one journal that covered maybe two or three months,
the last months…" Containing what we don't know

Following impulse, one voice gleaning from
another where volley is sometimes stranger

than that displayed in Stoppard's play: Rosencrantz
& Guildenstern lob questions across metaphorical net
that suggests game or trap, and the chasm between
is the felt distance readers must travel.

Thinking about Sylvia Plath
and Anne Sexton

About how they never got over pain,
considering the way child's loss
worked itself up 33 bones—
these vertebrae that form spine
—where sadness and loss lodged
in cells of dorsal root ganglia,
on route to the brain
where at will they could return
to seasons of girls
catching fire,
transmitting torment into
articulation.
No suicide girls, these women
who chose immolation
even though choice implies preference
when it is no more than opportunity
at slivered edge. These poets
let us hear noise beneath din,
those sounds we scarcely recognize,
overlapping as they are
by slapping sounds on water.
How to describe it exactly—
fluctuating quiver of emotion
moving emptiness, filling
void with desolation as we try
to find our way by echolocation,
listening, separating out cymbals
because, after all, it is just
air beating on inner ear,
asking to be let in.

This is the Beast
of our Violent Dreams

We might have been on safari
but were only fantasizing so
from an open-air vehicle
tumbling over manufactured
indentations and imperfections
in this perfectly conceived road.

So, when the rhino huffed into
our path and turned to stare us
down, we started, remembering
Kinsella's poem, and that rough
beast DÜrer gave immortality to
as its template sank beneath waves.

This is not the beast of our technology,
DÜrer's imaginings even then,
with hardware plating and horns worn
like war weapons; this is the beast of
our violent dreams. All its armor
sufficient to make the truck pull up

and hesitate, the motor grinding its
metal teeth, in nervous anticipation
as the rhino moved toward us at a
threatening pace, calling up another
geologic age, 32 million years ago,
from North American Wind Caves.

Anxiety that powerful translator
of this radical intensity encased
in fold after fold of scabrous skin,
and in those long moments, he
provided us another identity,
remembering we had invited the ride.

This beast of our violent dreams

was no five-star general about
to rend our braking vehicle in two,
but, rather, the ogre who surprises
at the end of night's
watch on a picket line.

There and then, we stalled—breathless, fully alive,
as the truck worked its protesting engine—
we awaited indifferent mercy.

Sometimes Loss Weighs Lightly

Absence
of hummingbird nest from thinnest
of pine branches overhanging the porch
where—if I sat quietly—
she would seem to spontaneously appear,
hover near my face,
dart sideways,
then settle onto lichen and spider silk nest

Two chicks spiked bills straight up,
like blackened toothpicks
jabbing air
until she arrived and offered bounty

Absence
nothing at all like the time I gathered photographs
of my father who lay in his coffin,
congratulating myself on how I'd held it together
until I picked up his Syracuse cap.

Nothing at all like my brother's deepest dive,
or the way I felt when the Sherriff had to break
windows in my aunt's house to find her body,
or my mother mouthing words no longer hers.

Two summers the hummingbird had come
and made her nest in my tree,
but I haven't seen her since.

Even if I waited patiently all day and night—
sometimes loss weighs lightly,
but it always weighs.

Red Tails

Winter is the season
when I see these birds of prey
in a different light, finding them resting
at the tops of bare-limbed trees, wind ruffling
their feathers, their red heads
drawn down; snow mixing with
white plumes on their breasts.

We have adopted the word *hawk* to mean warmonger
and chauvinist. Even the female of the species
is so characterized, without consideration
for her aerial displays, rather for her keen-eyed
violence at the end of a dive.

In spring, summer, and autumn,
the Red Tail Hawk is a high flyer, difficult
to spot up close, soaring over distant fields,
but in density of winter—with wind
swirling tornados of snow—Red Tails
shelter at edges of open fields,
scanning snow blankets for imperfections
and slight ripples that indicate a mouse,
mole, or vole.

I once saw the skin of a rabbit nearly
intact on a snow-covered meadow;
hunter leaving not even bones in its
exacting evisceration of creature
formerly housed by gray and white
fur, and I felt something akin to horror
for the brutality of the act,
yet, startlingly, also recognized kinship
not with ill-fated cony but with severe hawk.

Teacher to Her Student Whose Mother Died

I did not know your mother, who left you too soon,
but she must have been gentle
for the distinguishing mark on her son
is that of a gentle man.

I did not know your mother,
but she must have been wise
for the sage within you
lights a path.

I did not know your mother,
but she must have been kind
for an altruistic spirit
rounds your shoulders.

I did not know your mother,
but she must have been lovely
for an appreciation of the aesthetic
has been cultivated in you.

I did not know your mother,
but she must have been extraordinary
for her son stands tall as a scholar and exemplar
of all that is good and fine.

"…You May as Well Make [Them] Dance."
[George Bernard Shaw]

At the back of a Catholic church,
two long pews bore witness.
Shaw or Yeats preferred by this Queen
who leaned into secrets, theirs as well as her own.
This matriarch nearly died, the stroke
causing her to bend, but now she sat straight and tall
and believing, daughters
and granddaughters, sons and grandsons
surround her, this woman a center
of an Irish American, clamorous universe
commanding respect, if not for God
then for family. Here they would meet,
silent and knowing, on this Holy Night,
the members of a family of linemen, farmers,
nurses, foremen, lawyers, politicians,
beauticians, tree surgeons, administrators,
teachers, chefs, and carpenters.

Daughters held out for love, sons broke hearts
and were broken: brushes with death, accidents,
divorces, weddings, and births abound.
Red or raven-haired with high cheekbones
from their father's side, these exotic beauties
taken in by the matriarch's gaze simultaneously
fixed on the cross; her peripheral vision
adjusting to a two-year-old attempting
to reach her; she knew full well the tragic echoes
woven in her fabric, but on this blessed eve,
she understood they were sublime.

To Epiphany

Short Street of Memory

Astounded by the bob, drag,
disappearance of lure and end
of line, a child who should have
known better than to hold so lightly
her father's pole over racing water—

by the hot, rancid breath of angry bull
against her back as the girl
raced across open fields,
leaping and swinging
into waiting arms of a tree—

by the arc of brother's body
flying, sprung momentarily
from gravity's grave hold until released
from paralysis of diaphragm,
eyes shot through with amazement—

by the years between child
and child's keeper, the adult looking back
in wave after wave after wave
of current, impulse no longer
than the short street of memory

Child Who Would Not

Shapeless sleeping,
I dreamed of you,
mourning when you were not born,
holding your hand while I named trees:
there's African Baobab, Spanish Cedar,
European Ash, Japanese Maple, fiery red and gold,
the Maidenhair Tree, held sacred, with its cultivation of hope,
thin, Quaking Aspen, I point to, with its imploring arms
reaching upward, but it is the Kapok that interests you,
with its spreading roots guiding souls
of the dead; wait, I say, opening my throat
like the Australian Umbrella. If we could only
walk this world, I would point to the European
Black Elder with its connecting buds
like ganglia, but your interest lies
in the finely fissured
Tree of Heaven.

I come back again to Bristlecone Pine
in its barren landscape.
"Death sets a thing significant," wrote Dickinson,
yet outside birth and death obliquely you remain
while I cradle incomprehension until it settles
sometime in the middle of the night;
I never heard your breath but felt you
breathing. Ascending sun
troubles a cooled earth,
and an exhalation
suggests leaving.
Connected by sighs,
a long, thin cord conjoining
us, the umbilical flowering vine of memory.
You recede into that inner dark, my dissident child,
reversing process: born into me.

A Turning

Coming across primeval poems
I had written decades ago,
predating allusions—
still too young, too raw—
I tossed them into air,
recycling bin waiting at my bare feet,
my left toe knocking against it blindly
as images scrambled a moment,
suggesting consciousness
in the odd odors that infiltrate aged papers;
something about wood never quite
leaves.

Perusing my early poems, I decipher
young imagination seeing a fissure
left in blue by migrating geese,
indulgently suggesting sexuality:
darkness, water, waking—all personified
bodies tied to emerging sexual self,
overdone, dramatic to point that I smile,
tossing sheets of paper
like soiled bed linen.
Nowhere amongst those lines
do I find Rich's opus, Olson's polish,
not even the hint of Celestine Frost's restraint.

Dragging blue bin to the curb,
I leave remnants of younger self,
developing writer, in yesterday's garbage
huddled together to await morning.
At some point in the night, I stir,
dreaming of a girl, too anxious
to go back to sleep,
so, I slip outside with the dew,
before we are meant to wake,
to rummage through bin and rescue
poems of another lifetime.

When I lay them out to dry,
I brew coffee and brood, thinking,
"Someone else will have to rid the past."
I read lines again and remember.

Hope for Water Bears

At furthest edges of human destruction,
past the reach of cruel, manipulative politics
played out in bombed out cities, hateful racism,
misogyny, xenophobia, homophobia; close to atrocities
committed on women and children; beneath war drones,
past boundaries in a gun-fueled, nuclear-threatened,
man-altered world of the starving and desperate sinking
into utter hopelessness; we have the calm of the water bear,
the most indestructible species on our planet.

This little, eight-legged micro-animal
is believed to have survived cataclysm and will withstand
our own apocalyptic endings—take your pick—
likely surviving everything, really, except an extinguished sun.

"Moss piglets," or Tardigrade,
if you want to get scientific with naming, but it's likely
water bears don't care much for nomenclature,
human intervention in world affairs, wars, lies, hate.

They aren't very strong, but they can endure
a trip into outer space on the skin of a rocket ship
and back into our fiery atmosphere.
Only around 10 billion years of drawing in water
and lasting through dehydration in their desiccation state,
reminiscent of hibernation,
water bears are all about coming through.
No food or water for thirty years? They endure.

Not terribly attractive, water bears resemble
an Idaho potato gone soft, sprouting tiny claws.
Looking like miniature moles with rhino hide—
they have long, sunken slits where eyes would be
but are not likely to care about
our estimation of their beauty
as they burrow in the lowest parts of seas
or attach to highest mountains.

If we only speak of humanities' love, art, music, quest for knowledge, we might mistakenly pity the water bear.

Alchemy at Lac Yser

"There is gold all around," he said.

I return long after the gold mine closed
and my father died.
Inheriting his penchant for telling stories
and a little red cabin in Quebec,
I watch wind over water
propelling dark clouds,
heavy with burdens,
while I curl up in a blanket,
look out a rattled window
as the roof heaves and sighs
inside a cove with waving pines
and spindly white birch
come down to the water's edge
to lap at a wild deep lake long
with islets, islands, and sudden rises.

Like my father before me,
I hear wave after wave slapping shore
and see sun all around
turning leaves, sand, and water to gold.

Gemimor, Marth, Merimna

Nabokov titled his autobiography
as command: *Speak, Memory,*
and a thousand details convulse in little shocks and sadness.
When my mother lost her memory,
she lost herself but continued fighting.
Nothing but anguish at the bottom
of that endless well of affliction,
deeper losses, blocked synapses in her brain.

In an antique store in southern Virginia,
I moved carefully past brittleness:
china, mirrors, wine glasses,
fragile vessels of the past, until I discovered,
behind a pile of venerable books—
ones that dampness had started to rot
with mildew's black dots—
Don Quixote on his horse Rocinante.
A treasure exposed, but alas,
errant-knight was missing his lance
and Sancho Panza.
Still, this carved-by-hand wooden figure
possessed some magic,
some madness recalling Miguel de Cervantes'
novel and his characters
in which mind and mindfulness are fought for,
against impossible odds,
tragically, heroically with imagined lance
and insubstantial, yet elevated status.

Don Quixote came home with me
and took a place on my bookshelf
before being surrounded by thick tomes,
until rediscovery and dusting off time,
as we do from time to time.
Perhaps because memory allows us
to imperfectly revisit those we have lost,
those who are absent from our lives in present tense,

memory seems perpetually anointed
with inescapable sadness, all that history buried
within words from which memory arose:
an etymology of the word
from Welsh's *marth*, we have sorrow;
Old English, too, with *gemimor*
and *murnan*, remembering sorrowfully,
mourn and known,
these associations seeming to whisper
behind our word memory.

Closest we come to merging origins
of language and meaning,
memory retains its past lives;
offers awareness of recollection of Greek's
merimna, meaning thought, causing anxiety,
just as enfeebled Alonso Quixano caused such
to poor Sancho Panza who instinctively
knew that he was blessed, not cursed,
to have met that crazy old man.

All We've Been Through

This tension in the allure of encountering words
unfamiliar to travelers or hosts, this foreign pilgrim
coming from an unknown city in a world,
it is said, of private streets and coded houses
in which we hope to engage
with characters elegant or coarse,
memorable or easily forgotten
in the moment of accidental or deliberate collisions.

With window lights always in the distance,
no matter how far or fast we proceed on foot,
we hope to come to concurrence.

We've been talking and writing
in the language of trees
with stems and branches, roots and base of morphology,
but our roots suddenly lift up out of the soil
and stride as we move out over the world,
nomadic, searching.

Explorers or migrants, tourists or vagrants,
it matters the matter you came
to discuss and from where you came,
what you are named,
and why you are heading out over landscapes.

All we've been through to find again strangeness
in this part of town, we used to call home.
If there is to be communion, it will be back lit
in our neural circuity
and recounted fondly, sadly, in past tense.

Even mistakes and mistaken encounters—
heart-breaking with fluttering lexemes
of singular, false notes drifting down
from our desire to commune,
to make in common but never common.

W riter, poet, and educator **Nancy Avery Dafoe** has published poetry and prose, books on teaching writing *Breaking Open the Box* and *Writing Creatively: A Guided Journal* through Rowman & Littlefield Education (2013 and 2014, respectively); a book on policy, *The Misdirection of Education Policy: Raising Questions about School Reform*, also through Rowman & Littlefield (2016). A chapbook of poetry, *Poets Diving in the Night* (2016) and this book *The Innermost Sea*, through Finishing Line Press. A cross-genre memoir and book of poetry, *An Iceberg in Paradise: A Passage through Alzheimer's* was published through SUNY Press (2015). Her novels *You Enter a Room* and *Both End in Speculation*, part of a literary murder mystery series, were published through Rogue Phoenix Press (2017 and 2018).

Dafoe's poems, essays, and stories have appeared in numerous literary publications and won awards locally and nationally, including the William Faulkner/William Wisdom creative writing contest in poetry (2016). *Poets Diving in the Night* was one of three finalists in the Central New York Book Awards in 2017. Her fiction and non-fiction work also appear in the anthologies *Lost Orchard*, published by SUNY Press (2014) and in *New York Votes for Women: A Suffrage Centennial Anthology* (2017), among other publications. She is a member of the National League of American Pen Women, Inc. (NLAPW).

She lives in Homer, New York with her husband Daniel, son Blaise, and dog Bogie. She has two daughters Colette and Nicole, sons-in-law Dave and Adam, and four grandsons, Truman, Enzo, Owen, and Luca for whom she is eternally grateful.

www.ingramcontent.com/pod-product-compliance
Lightning Source LLC
Chambersburg PA
CBHW021154090426

42740CB00008B/1090

9 7 8 1 6 3 5 3 4 7 9 9 9